Cool Cars

JAGUAR

BY DALTON RAINS

WWW.APEXEDITIONS.COM

Copyright © 2026 by Apex Editions, Mendota Heights, MN 55120. All rights reserved. No part of this book may be reproduced or utilized in any form or by any means without written permission from the publisher.

Apex is distributed by North Star Editions:
sales@northstareditions.com | 888-417-0195

Produced for Apex by Red Line Editorial.

Photographs ©: Pexels, cover; Shutterstock Images, 1, 12, 13, 16–17, 18, 19, 20–21, 26–27, 29; Jaguar Racing/Getty Images Sport/Getty Images, 4–5, 8–9; Vince Mignott/MB Media/Getty Images Sport/Getty Images, 6–7; National Motor Museum/Heritage Images/Hulton Archive/Getty Images, 10–11; iStockphoto, 14–15; Spencer Platt/Getty Images News/Getty Images, 22–23; Neilson Barnard/Jaguar Land Rover/Getty Images Entertainment/Getty Images, 24–25

Library of Congress Control Number: 2024952632

ISBN
979-8-89250-521-5 (hardcover)
979-8-89250-557-4 (paperback)
979-8-89250-628-1 (ebook pdf)
979-8-89250-593-2 (hosted ebook)

Printed in the United States of America
Mankato, MN
082025

NOTE TO PARENTS AND EDUCATORS

Apex books are designed to build literacy skills in striving readers. Exciting, high-interest content attracts and holds readers' attention. The text is carefully leveled to allow students to achieve success quickly. Additional features, such as bolded glossary words for difficult terms, help build comprehension.

TABLE OF CONTENTS

CHAPTER 1
CHAMPIONS 4

CHAPTER 2
HISTORY 10

CHAPTER 3
MODERN JAGUARS 16

CHAPTER 4
RARE MODELS 22

COMPREHENSION QUESTIONS • 28
GLOSSARY • 30
TO LEARN MORE • 31
ABOUT THE AUTHOR • 31
INDEX • 32

CHAPTER 1

CHAMPIONS

It's the last race of the 2024 Formula E season. Mitch Evans drives a Jaguar. Nick Cassidy does, too. Their cars speed around the track.

Jaguar drivers Mitch Evans (left) and Nick Cassidy (right) race in Formula E's 2024 London E-Prix.

Other cars close in on Evans. So, he presses a button. His Jaguar goes into Attack Mode. It gives him a speed boost. The electric car streaks ahead.

Formula E is a racing series for electric cars.

ATTACK MODE

Drivers can use Attack Mode twice in each race. Drivers press a button. Then they drive along a specific part of the track. Driving there takes a bit longer. But it lets them gain extra power and speed for a short time.

Both Jaguars zoom across the finish line. Evans places second. Cassidy comes in third. That's all they need. Jaguar wins the Formula E Team Championship!

FAST FACT

In Formula E, the team with the most points after the season wins the Team Championship.

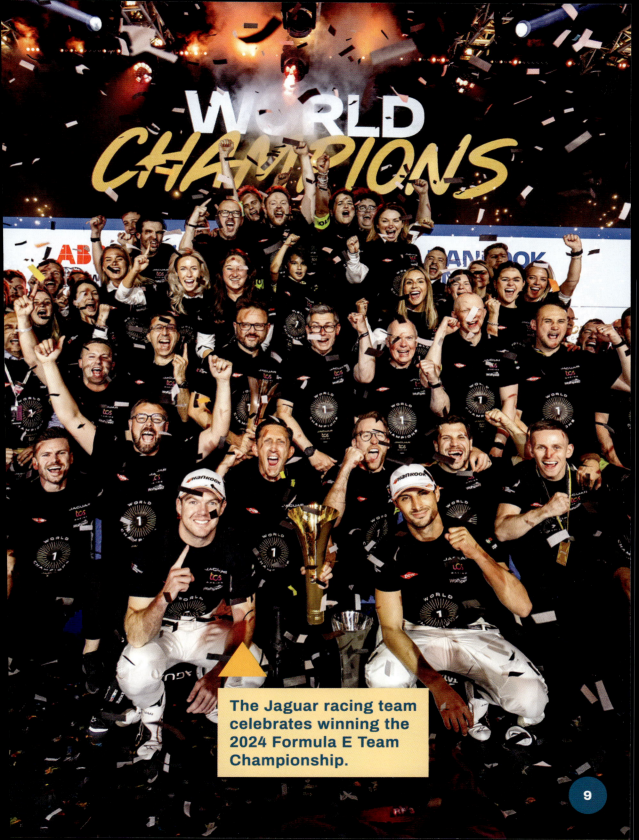

The Jaguar racing team celebrates winning the 2024 Formula E Team Championship.

CHAPTER 2

History

In 1922, William Lyons started a company. He made **sidecars** for motorcycles. The company released its first cars in the 1930s.

William Lyons changed the company's name to Jaguar in 1945.

In 1948, the XK120 was the world's fastest road-legal car.

In 1948, the XK120 helped make Jaguar known for speed. The C-Type and D-Type built off the XK120. But new **chassis** made them faster. Both models won many races in the 1950s.

E-Types

In 1961, Jaguar released the E-Type. It had a long body and shiny **accents**. The **design** was unlike any other car. It was a huge success.

Many people said pictures of the E-Type didn't fully show how beautiful the car was.

In the late 1900s and early 2000s, Jaguar built many new **luxury** cars. They blended the company's history of racing with **elegant** designs.

FAST FACT
The XJ220 was the fastest Jaguar ever. It set a speed record at 217 miles per hour (349 km/h).

Jaguar built XJ220s from 1992 to 1994. Fewer than 300 were ever made.

CHAPTER 3

MODERN JAGUARS

Jaguar made many popular models in the 2000s. The first Jaguar XF came out in 2007. The car's body looked modern. It had sharp angles.

Jaguar became known for its cars' wire mesh grilles.

The F-Type was Jaguar's first two-seat car in 50 years.

Jaguar F-Types first came out in 2012. These cars had smoother curves than the XF models. The two-seat cars looked sportier, too. Some had open tops.

SPORTBRAKES

XFR-S Sportbrakes looked different from other Jaguars. The station wagons had long roofs. The backs were roomy. But the cars still had loud, powerful engines.

The XFR-S Sportbrake could hit 60 miles per hour (97 km/h) in 4.6 seconds.

Jaguar's first SUVs sold in 2016. Like other Jaguars, the SUVs had polished accents and sporty designs. They used fancy materials, too.

FAST FACT
In the mid-2020s, Jaguar decided to stop making gasoline-powered vehicles. It began the shift to all-electric cars.

The F-Pace SUV was one of Jaguar's top sellers through the early 2020s.

CHAPTER 4
RARE MODELS

Jaguar came out with several rare cars. The XKR-S GT arrived in 2013. It was built like a race car. But drivers could also take it on the road.

Jaguar built only 45 XKR-S GTs.

Jaguar made only 250 F-Type Project 7s. The sports cars showed off open tops and rear wings. These features were designed to look like Jaguar D-Types.

Project 8s

The XE SV Project 8 was another speedy car. It could rocket faster than 200 miles per hour (320 km/h). Jaguar made 300 Project 8s.

Jaguar's Project 8 (left) came out in 2017. The Project 7 (right) was released three years before.

The C-X75 was a **concept car**. Its **hybrid** engine looked to the future. But the car was beautiful like Jaguars before it. It showed how the carmaker remained great.

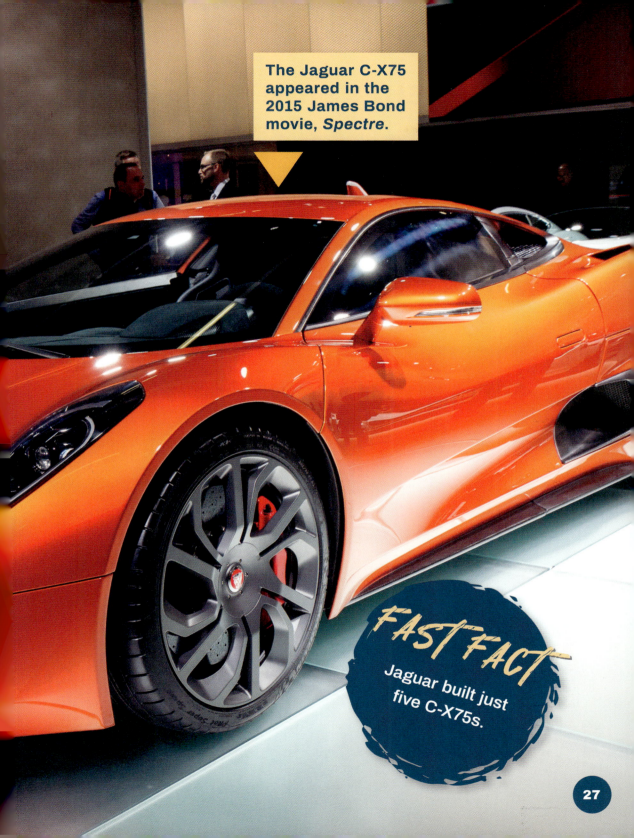

The Jaguar C-X75 appeared in the 2015 James Bond movie, *Spectre*.

FAST FACT
Jaguar built just five C-X75s.

COMPREHENSION QUESTIONS

Write your answers on a separate piece of paper.

1. Write a few sentences explaining the main ideas of Chapter 2.

2. Which Jaguar model would you most like to have? Why?

3. When did the Jaguar XK120 come out?
    - A. 1922
    - B. 1948
    - C. 1961

4. How could Jaguar win a Formula E championship without winning in the last race of the 2024 season?
    - A. Other teams had more points than Jaguar.
    - B. Points from only the last race mattered.
    - C. Points from every race in the season mattered.

5. What does **boost** mean in this book?

*It gives him a speed **boost**. The electric car streaks ahead.*

- **A.** an increase in speed
- **B.** a decrease in speed
- **C.** a new car

6. What does **blended** mean in this book?

*They **blended** the company's history of racing with elegant designs.*

- **A.** did not use
- **B.** brought together
- **C.** kept apart

Answer key on page 32.

GLOSSARY

accents
Markings that stand out, often using bright colors.

chassis
Parts of cars that support their weight. They are often the frames.

concept car
A vehicle that shows new technologies or designs.

design
The way things look or are made.

elegant
Very graceful and grand.

hybrid
Able to use two different sources of energy, such as gas and electricity.

luxury
Having to do with things that are high quality, comfortable, and often expensive.

sidecars
Small, low vehicles attached to the sides of motorcycles.

TO LEARN MORE

BOOKS
Morey, Allan. *Inventing Cars*. Focus Readers, 2022.
Rusick, Jessica. *Electric Cars*. Abdo Publishing, 2024.
Woodland, Faith. *Jaguar*. AV2, 2022.

ONLINE RESOURCES
Visit **www.apexeditions.com** to find links and resources related to this title.

ABOUT THE AUTHOR
Dalton Rains is a writer and editor from St. Paul, Minnesota.

C
C-Type, 12
C-X75, 26–27
Cassidy, Nick, 4, 8

D
D-Type, 12, 24

E
E-Type, 13
Evans, Mitch, 4, 6, 8

F
F-Type, 18
F-Type Project 7, 24
Formula E, 4, 6–8

L
Lyons, William, 10

X
XE SV Project 8, 25
XF, 16, 18
XFR-S Sportbrake, 19
XJ220, 15
XK120, 12
XKR-S GT, 22

ANSWER KEY:
1. Answers will vary; 2. Answers will vary; 3. B; 4. C; 5. A; 6. B